What's Worrying you?

Molly Potter

ILLUSTRATED BY Sarah Jennings

FEATHERSTONE
AN IMPRINT OF BLOOMSBURY
LONDON OXFORD NEW YORK NEW DELHI SYDNEY

For my wonderful friend Sallyann
who makes light work of worries and is fantastic at perspective.

Featherstone Education
An imprint of Bloomsbury Publishing Plc

50 Bedford Square
London
WC1B 3DP
UK

1385 Broadway
New York
NY 10018
USA

www.bloomsbury.com

FEATHERSTONE and the Feather logo are trademarks of Bloomsbury Publishing Plc

First published in Great Britain 2018

Text © Molly Potter 2018
Illustrations © Sarah Jennings 2018

A catalogue record for this book is available from the British Library.

Library of Congress Cataloguing-in-Publication data has been applied for.

ISBN
HB: 978 1 4729 4980 6
ePDF: 978 1 4729 4981 3

2 4 6 8 10 9 7 5 3

Printed and bound in China by Leo Paper Products, Heshan, Guangdong

This book is produced using paper that is made from wood grown in managed, sustainable forests.
It is natural, renewable and recyclable. The logging and manufacturing processes conform to the
environmental regulations of the country of origin.

To find out more about our authors and books visit www.bloomsbury.com. Here you will find extracts,
author interviews, details of forthcoming events and the option to sign up for our newsletters.

Dear Reader,

Before you delve into this book, just remember that EVERYONE worries about things – even grownups! You could say that worries are unhelpful thoughts that go round and round in your head and make you feel negative emotions like being sad, angry, jealous, embarrassed and (of course) worried! Sometimes these emotions can confuse us and leave us not knowing what to think or do.

This book is about all sorts of things that children might worry about. It looks at each worry in turn and then considers how that worry might make you feel and what you might think. There are lots of suggestions for things you can think about and actions you can take to make you feel better and stop worrying so much!

It's good to know...

...that it's perfectly normal to worry and that certain things bother some people more than others. Most of the time, worries come and then they go. It's when a worry gets really stuck for a long time or begins to affect your life that things become serious. So, if something is worrying you that this book doesn't help with and you can't sort it out by yourself, you need to talk to adults you trust until one of them helps you find a solution.

What's in this book...

When you get told off...

When you get a new teacher...

When you see something horrible on TV...

When you find something difficult...

When you fall out with a friend...

When someone picks on you...

When your
parents argue...

Turn to page 18.

When you are scared
of things that are not
dangerous – like spiders
or the dark...

Turn to page 20.

When someone
else has something
you want...

Turn to page 22.

When you feel nobody
is listening to you...

Turn to page 24.

When you don't have
friends to play with...

Turn to page 26.

When you get ill...

Turn to page 28.

When you get told off...

How you might feel

★ Tearful ★ Angry ★ Guilty
★ Embarrassed ★ In a panic
★ Ashamed ★ Misunderstood
★ Shocked ★ Annoyed

What you might be thinking

It's not fair.

I didn't mean to do it.

But I only did it because...

I wasn't the only one.
Other people did it too.

When you get told off, try and find out what you need to do to make things better.

Think about what you did. Did it harm anyone or anything? What could you do to put it right?

I need to buy you another pencil.

Do you need to say sorry to someone? (This will probably make you and the other person feel better.)

Sorry.

Things to remember...

Stop playing that. I have a bad head!

Was the person who told you off having a bad day? (This is sometimes why children get told off. It's not fair but adults don't get things right all the time.)

Sometimes it helps if you explain exactly what happened and why you did what you did. (It's best to do this when everyone is calm.)

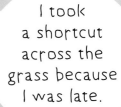

I took a shortcut across the grass because I was late.

When you get a new teacher...

How you might feel

★ Sad ★ Anxious ★ Upset
★ Insecure ★ Worried
★ Uncertain ★ Nervous
★ Butterflies in your tummy

What you might be thinking

But I liked my old teacher.

I don't know the new teacher.

What if the new teacher is horrible?

I like things to stay the same.

When you get a new teacher, say hello and smile the first time you meet them. They might be nervous too.

We don't sit on the carpet now we're in Year 1.

When something changes, we worry that we'll lose the things we like and there'll be new things we don't like.

We often worry about changes more than we need to. It might only take a few days to get used to a new teacher.

I like our new teacher now.

Things to remember...

Having different teachers in each class makes school more interesting and gives us lots of different experiences.

There will be lots of things your new teacher does that you'll like a lot.

Look Mum, I got a sticker from my new teacher.

When you see something horrible on TV...

How you might feel

★ Worried ★ Sad ★ Scared
★ Confused ★ Stressed
★ Shocked ★ In a panic

What you might be thinking

Is it something that might happen to me?

Does that happen a lot?

Is that real?

Why did it happen?

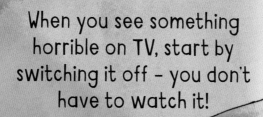

When you see something horrible on TV, start by switching it off - you don't have to watch it!

Remember that what happens on TV isn't always real.

When you see something shocking, it can be scary and stay in your head going round and round. If that happens talk to an adult you trust.

I can't help thinking about that nasty monster.

Things to remember...

Remember to stay where you can touch the bottom.

Your parents/carers and teachers do lots of things to keep you safe and away from some of the dangerous things that you might see on TV.

The News reports the most shocking events from all over the world. Most things in the News are happening a long way away.

When you **find something difficult**...

How you might feel

★ Frustrated ★ Confused
★ Irritated ★ Disappointed
★ Sad ★ Obsessed ★ Stressed

What you might be thinking

Why do other people seem to find this easy? It's not fair.

I must be rubbish.

I found it really hard last time too.

I really wish I found it easy.

When you find something difficult, you could decide to be really determined to get good at whatever it is.

Try not to get cross or give up when things don't go right the first time. Sometimes you need to try really hard, and to do that you need to stay calm.

Don't forget – everybody has things they are good at and things they are not so good at. It's good to think about all the things you do well and celebrate your achievements.

Things to remember...

Practising things always helps you get better at them. Some things take a long time to get good at.

Ask for help – there is usually someone who can help you get better at something.

When you **fall out with a friend...**

How you might feel

★ Angry ★ Misunderstood
★ Sad ★ Disappointed
★ Distrustful ★ Lonely
★ Confused ★ Ignored

What you might be thinking

I'll never be friends with them again.

They didn't understand what I was trying to do or say.

They've been unfair and unkind.

I hate him/her.

When you fall out with a friend, spend some time away from them while you think about what to do next.

Friends often fall out with each other but don't worry, things can nearly always be sorted out so you can be friends again.

I want us to be friends again.

Remember you were friends before you fell out and that there are still lots of reasons why you like each other.

Things to remember...

Understand that you and your friend are probably seeing what happened in completely different ways.

I really wanted to come to the park but my mum made me tidy my bedroom.

I thought you didn't like me anymore because you didn't come.

A PLAN FOR MAKING UP

1. Ask your friend if you can talk together alone.

2. Say clearly that you want to make up.

3. Take turns to speak and listen carefully. Both explain what made you fall out.

4. Find out what needs to happen for you to both feel better again.

5. Say sorry for any upset you caused.

6. Keep talking until you are both happy with each other.

15

When **someone** picks on you...

How you might feel
- ★ Angry ★ Helpless
- ★ Scared ★ Nervous
- ★ Lonely ★ In a panic
- ★ Sad ★ Annoyed

You can't play, you're no good!

What you might be thinking

Leave me alone.

You're horrible.

That's really unfair. I haven't been nasty to you.

I'll get you back.

When someone picks on you,
try really hard to stop yourself
from just being nasty back.

16

Big nose.

Yes, I know it's enormous.

If someone teases you, try agreeing with them and see what happens. They really won't know what to say because they won't be expecting you to agree!

Remember that people often pick on other people because they think it will make them feel better. This can be because they are actually quite grumpy or unhappy themselves.

I bet you haven't got any friends.

Things to remember...

He was really mean.

Tell good friends what happened and how it made you feel. Let your friends help cheer you up!

If someone picks on you on purpose more than once and you feel you can't sort it out yourself, this is bullying and you need to tell an adult you trust until somebody makes it stop.

BULLYING

17

When your **parents argue...**

How you might feel

★ Sad ★ Scared
★ Worried ★ Grumpy
★ Helpless ★ Ignored
★ Angry ★ Unloved

What you might be thinking

I want them to stop – I can't bear this.

I don't want them to split up.

I want to be somewhere else.

Have they forgotten about me and how this makes me feel?

When your parents argue, tell them how it's making you feel.

Arguing can be a noisy way of sorting out a problem.

You do the washing.

Can't you do it for once?

When people argue they are taken over by their emotions. This can make them say things they don't mean.

You're the most annoying person I know.

Things to remember...

I'm sorry - I was just in a bad mood earlier.

That's OK.

Nearly everyone's parents have arguments sometimes but most arguments end with parents making up.

If your parents start to make each other unhappy more than they make each other happy, then they may decide to split up. This can bring about lots of change but after a while things will start to feel normal again.

Have a good time with Mum.

19

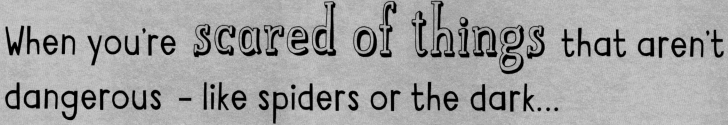

When you're **scared of things** that aren't dangerous - like spiders or the dark...

How you might feel

★ Scared ★ Nervous ★ Jumpy
★ In a panic ★ Uncertain
★ Insecure ★ Frightened

What you might
be thinking

I'm too scared to move.

I know this is silly but I can't help it.

I can't look.

I want to run.

When you're
scared of something,
think of things that
make you smile.

Whatever is scaring you isn't going to harm you at all. It simply can't!

No monsters under there, don't be silly.

You can make the scary thing seem ridiculous by singing a funny or cheerful song.

Silly banging and flashing in the sky, Indoors I stay safe and dry.

Things to remember...

I'm safe. I'm safe. I AM safe!

Although you might feel scared, there is really nothing to worry about so try saying 'I'm safe, I'm safe' in really silly voices until you make yourself laugh.

You can always go to a place where you feel really safe – that might be cuddling a parent or snuggled up in bed. When you feel safe, think about what scared you. Does it seem as scary now?

21

When someone else has something you want...

How you might feel

★ Envious ★ Jealous ★ Cross
★ Wistful ★ Inadequate
★ Resentful ★ Annoyed

What you might be thinking

I really, really, really want what they've got.

I wish I were them.

It's not fair.

I'm not good enough.

Wow! Your coat is amazing.

When you feel envious, tell yourself that you are GREAT. It can make you feel better.

22

My favourite colour is red.

Mine too.

This world would be a really boring place if everyone was the same.

And me!

I like being me.

Don't spend time comparing yourself with others. Enjoy being you!

Things to remember...

But I want more cake.

If you always get everything you want you probably won't be a very nice person, as you only think about your needs and not other people's.

Things aren't always fair and we can't change that. What we can do is change how we think and be grateful for all the things that are good in our lives.

I love my: mummy, teddy, bedroom, Saturdays with dad, pet rabbit, bicycle...

When you feel **nobody is listening to you...**

How you might feel

- ★ Frustrated ★ Helpless
- ★ Disappointed ★ Sad
- ★ Unimportant ★ Resentful
- ★ Tearful ★ Unloved

What you might be thinking

Please stop ignoring me.

What I have to say is really important.

I want adults to understand.

Why don't adults always listen to children?

When nobody is listening, be patient and wait until someone is ready to listen.

I need help please, I need help please, I need help!

If you need an adult to hear something – keep telling them until they listen.

Dad?

Not now. Tell me later.

When adults don't listen it's usually because they are really busy or stressed. When this happens, try again later.

Things to remember...

When you tell someone something that you really want them to hear, start by saying, 'this is really important to me even if it doesn't seem important to you'.

If you really want an adult to know something – you could try writing them a note or getting someone to help you write one.

This is really important to me. I want to know how to spell.

butafol   beatoful
beautifull

Dear Mum

25

When you don't have friends to play with...

How you might feel

★ Miserable ★ Lonely
★ Unloved ★ Bored ★ Hurt
★ Inadequate ★ Unimportant

What you might be thinking

Why won't anyone play with me?

I want to be liked.

I feel really sorry for myself.

I need someone to come and ask me to play.

When you don't have friends to play with, don't just sit around feeling sorry for yourself, as that won't solve anything.

Sometimes you can get left out just because nobody notices you're on your own.

When we start feeling sad, we can often get carried away with thoughts that make us feel worse like 'nobody likes me'. Remember – these are just in your head and not real.

I have no friends.

Things to remember...

Do you want to play catch?

There are probably other children somewhere nearby who don't have anyone to play with. Have a good look round for them and ask them to play.

Always play fairly. Children don't like playing with cheats!

1... 2... 3... 4...

When you get ill...

How you might feel

★ Sad ★ Uncomfortable

★ Miserable ★ Tired

★ Fed up ★ Irritated

What you might be thinking

I can't wait to feel better.

I feel awful.

I'm missing out.

This is boring.

When you get ill, go to bed and have lots of rest.

28

Try to get some sleep.

Most people are ill every now and then but it doesn't usually take long to get better.

I'm feeling better already.

Don't forget your body is very good at fighting bugs and other nasty illnesses.

Things to remember...

If you drink plenty of water and eat fruit and vegetables, it can make getting ill less likely.

When you're ill, it's nice to snuggle up on the sofa under a duvet and watch TV.

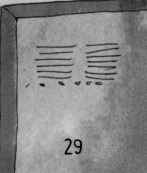

Feelings Glossary

Feeling	Description	An example of when you might feel it
Angry	When something has happened to make you really cross. You often feel tense, clench your fists and grit your teeth when you're angry.	If someone shoved you in the back for no reason when you were standing in a queue.
Anxious	When you're really worried or panicked (your heart beats fast) about something because you don't know what's going to happen.	If you have just been told you have to walk to your friend's house on your own because of an emergency and you're not sure you know the way.
Ashamed	When you feel bad about something you did that caused harm.	If you broke something that belonged to your mum but then lied about it and then your mum told you how special the thing was and you felt guilty about lying.
Disappointed	The feeling you have when you really wanted something to happen and then it didn't.	If you were really hoping for a pet for your birthday and then realised you weren't getting one.
Embarrassed	When you feel like you have done something that other people would laugh at or think you were silly for doing.	If you walked into a room and realised that your underpants were showing.
Envious	When someone else has something that you really, really want so that you feel sad every time you think about it.	If someone came into school with new trainers that you would really love to own or if a friend was really good looking and you wanted to look like him or her.
Frustrated	The feeling of getting really annoyed because you can't do something or achieve success.	If you were trying really hard to ice skate but you kept falling over.
Guilty	When you have done something wrong and you feel the shame of having done it.	If you took a cupcake from the kitchen and then you realised your parent had baked the exact number for the people he or she works with.
Helpless	When you feel like you simply cannot sort out a situation and you're not helping yourself at all.	If you were trying to make your upset friend feel better but they just kept crying.
Hurt	When someone has done something to upset you or caused you to become sad.	If someone who you liked said something nasty about you behind your back and you found out what they said.

Feeling	Description	An example of when you might feel it
Inadequate	When you feel like you're not good enough to do what needs to be done.	When you try hard to help your parent tidy up but you seem to be making more of a mess.
Insecure	When you feel uncertain, not confident and totally not sure of yourself.	If you were going to stay away from home for a few nights and you didn't know the people you were going to stay with.
Jealous	Very like being envious but normally about your feelings for another person.	If your good friend started spending more time with someone else than they spent with you.
Miserable	When you feel really, really sad and your world seems like a gloomy place.	If the pet you loved a lot just died.
Misunderstood	When someone doesn't get what you mean for some time.	If you said something that you thought was funny and entertaining and your friend decided you were being mean.
Nervous	When you don't feel sure at all and are a little scared to continue because you really don't know if you can do whatever you are about to do.	If you were to try walking a tightrope for the first time.
Obsessed	When you can't stop thinking about something – to the point that it really bothers you.	If you didn't win a competition and because you really wanted the prize, it keeps going round and round in your head.
Panicked	When you very suddenly feel fear usually caused by a thought or something in front of you and you stop thinking clearly and find it difficult to know what to do.	If you had just learned that your teacher was furious with you and you can see them marching towards you.
Resentful	When you feel cross with someone because you feel they treated you unfairly or badly.	If a teacher told you off for something you didn't do.
Stressed	When something that you don't like is strongly in your mind a lot of the time and making you feel tense and jumpy.	If you were really worried about something that was going to happen at school the following day like a test or something you're scared you won't be able to do.
Unloved	When you feel like you're not loved or nobody cares about you.	If your parents forgot your birthday (unlikely!).
Wistful	When you really long for something and feel sad or regret that you don't have it.	If you couldn't find a toy you used to really love and it seems to have gone missing.

A brief guide to helping your child talk about their worries

★ Spend time talking to your child about what exactly worrying is and how it might make them feel.

★ Always acknowledge your child's worries, even if they seem trivial to you. (As far as your child is concerned, this is proof you care.)

★ Explain to your child that worrying is normal and that most people worry at some point in their lives.

★ Help your child feel comfortable about discussing their worries openly. (Sharing worries with a trusted person can make the worry feel less daunting.)

★ Allow time to talk through any worries your child might have. Try not to jump in with solutions. Ask questions until you fully understand the situation and help your child come up with their own solutions by talking it through with them.

★ Explain that there are often some practical solutions to help deal with most worries, but another way of helping is to look at those worries differently. For example:

  ★ Ask your child to see if they can remember a time they were worried in the past and how this worry was eventually resolved.

  ★ Ask your child to imagine themselves as an adult and see if they think they would still be worrying about this (this can adjust perspective).

  ★ Allow some time for exploring the worry and then try and encourage your child to 'park' it if they can.

  ★ Ask your child to imagine the worry and then picture it getting smaller and smaller and eventually going away altogether.

What is worrying?

Worrying can be…

★ thoughts going round and round in your head about something that is really bothering you and causes negative emotions.

★ thinking about the future and fearing that it will be awful – even though it's likely to turn out fine.

★ feeling different physical sensations (e.g. unable to sleep, fast heartbeat, feeling tense in your tummy).